Disney

Songs of the 2000s

TENOR OR BARITONE

Recorded
Accompaniments
Online

To access recorded accompaniments online, visit:
www.halleonard.com/mylibrary

"Enter Code"
7714-4076-7114-7556

ISBN 978-1-5400-9666-1

Characters and Artwork © Disney

Visit Hal Leonard Online at
www.halleonard.com

Contact us:
Hal Leonard
7777 West Bluemound Road
Milwaukee, WI 53213
Email: info@halleonard.com

In Europe, contact:
Hal Leonard Europe Limited
42 Wigmore Street
Marylebone, London, W1U 2RN
Email: info@halleonardeurope.com

In Australia, contact:
Hal Leonard Australia Pty. Ltd.
4 Lentara Court
Cheltenham, Victoria, 3192 Australia
Email: info@halleonard.com.au

CONTENTS

All accompaniments performed by Brendan Fox except:
"Proud of Your Boy," performed by Richard Walters
"In Summer," performed by Ruben Piirainen

HOW TO USE HAL LEONARD ONLINE AUDIO

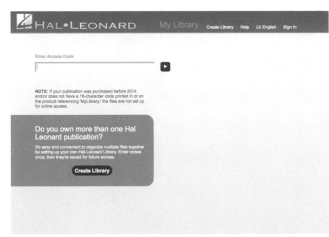

Because of the changing use of media, and the fact that fewer people are using CDs, we have made a shift to companion audio accessible online. In many cases, rather than a book with CD, we now have a book with an access code for online audio, including performances, accompaniments or diction lessons. Each copy of each book has a unique access code. We call this Hal Leonard created system "My Library." It's simple to use.

Go to www.halleonard.com/mylibrary and enter the unique access code found on page one of a relevant book/audio package.

The audio tracks can be streamed or downloaded. If you download the tracks on your computer, you can add the files to a CD or to your digital music library, and use them anywhere without being online. See below for comments about Apple and Android mobile devices.

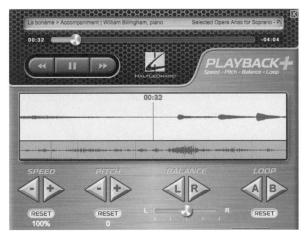

There are some great benefits to the My Library system. *Playback+* is exclusive to Hal Leonard, and when connected to the Internet with this multi-functional audio player you can:

• Change tempo without changing pitch
• Transpose to any key

Optionally, you can create a My Library account, and store all the companion audio you have purchased there. Access your account online at any time, from any device, by logging into your account at www.halleonard.com/mylibrary. Technical help may be found at www.halleonard.com/mylibrary/help/

Apple/iOS

Question: On my iPad and iPhone, the Download links just open another browser tab and play the track. How come this doesn't really download?

Answer: The Safari iOS browser will not allow you to download audio files directly in iTunes or other apps. There are several ways to work around this:

- You can download normally on your desktop computer, saving the files to iTunes. Then, you can sync your iOS device directly to your computer, or sync your iTunes content using an iCloud account.
- There are many third-party apps which allow you to download files from websites into the app's own file manager for easy retrieval and playback.

Android

Files are always downloaded to the same location, which is a folder usually called "Downloads" (this may vary slightly depending on what browser is used (Chrome, Firefox, etc)). Chrome uses a system app called "Downloads" where files can be accessed at any time. Firefox and some other browsers store downloaded files within a "Downloads" folder in the browser itself.

Recently-downloaded files can be accessed from the Notification bar; swiping down will show the downloaded files as a new "card", which you tap on to open. Opening a file depends on what apps are installed on the Android device. Audio files are opened in the device's default audio app. If a file type does not have a default app assigned to it, the Android system alerts the user.

I NEVER PLANNED ON YOU

from *Newsies The Musical*

Music by Alan Menken
Lyrics by Jack Feldman

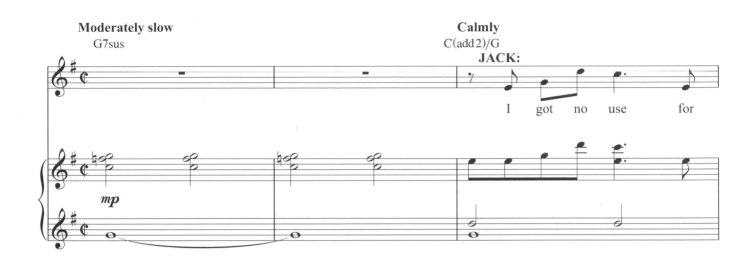

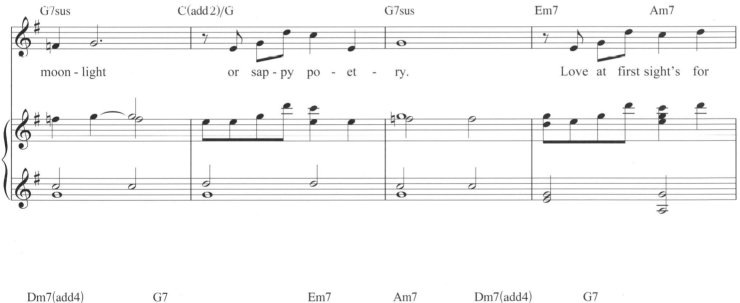

This has been adapted as a solo, eliminating "Don't Come A-Knocking."

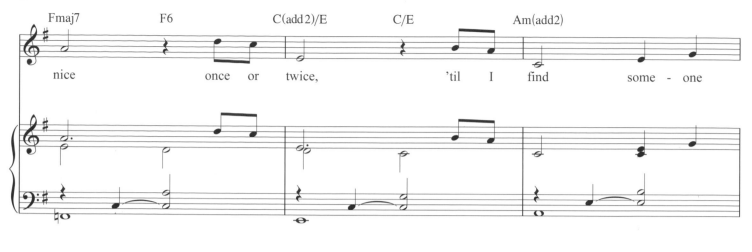

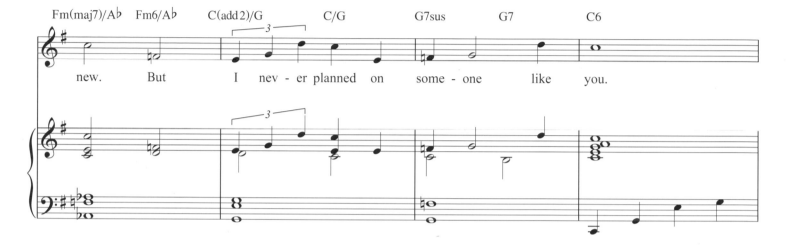

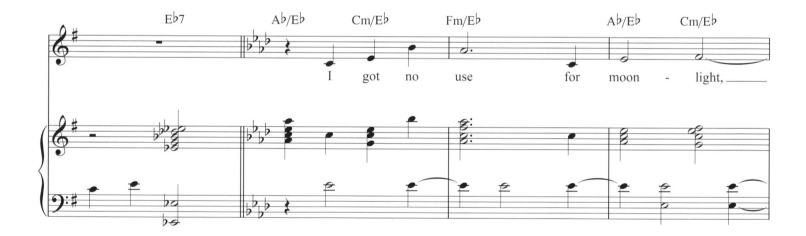

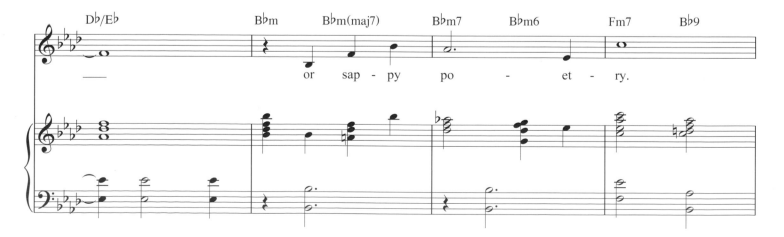

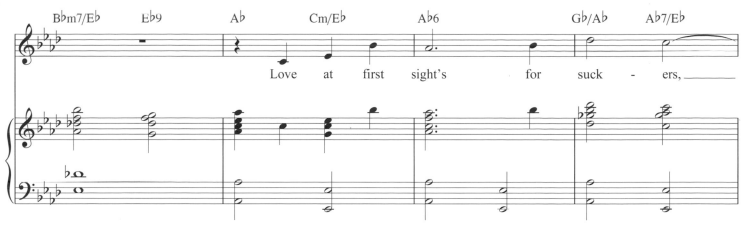

Love at first sight's for suck-ers, ___

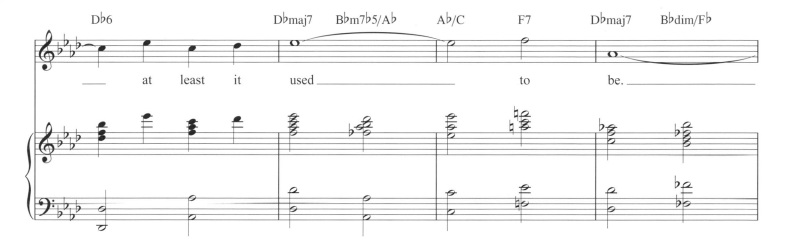

___ at least it used ___ to be. ___

No, I nev-er planned on some-

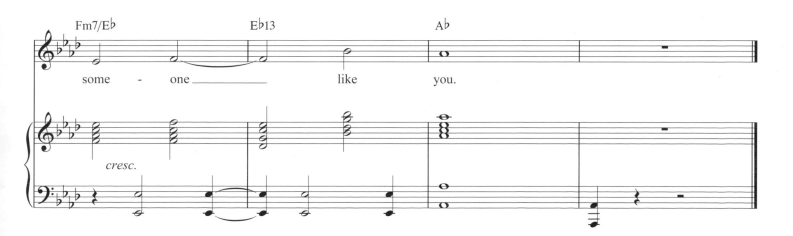

some-one ___ like you.

PROUD OF YOUR BOY

from *Aladdin*

Music by Alan Menken
Lyrics by Howard Ashman

With determination, poco rubato

ALADDIN:
Proud of your boy,

I'll make you proud of your boy. Be- lieve me,

Bad as I've been, Ma, you're in for a pleas- ant sur- prise.

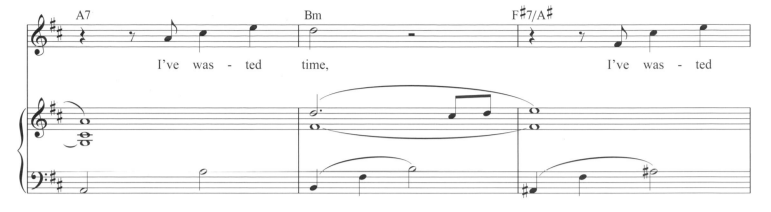

I've was-ted time, I've was-ted

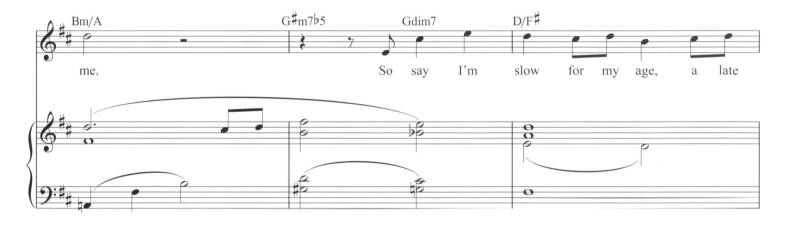

me. So say I'm slow for my age, a late

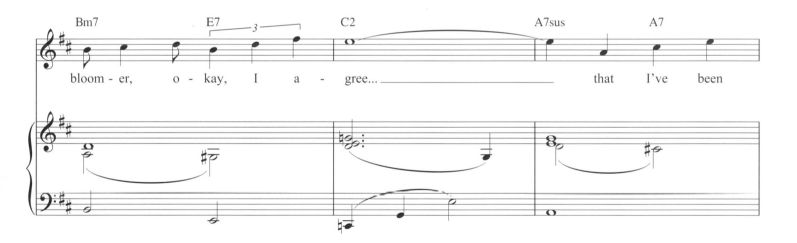

bloom-er, o-kay, I a-gree... that I've been

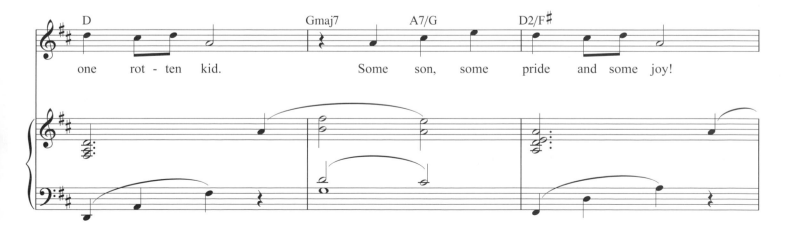

one rot-ten kid. Some son, some pride and some joy!

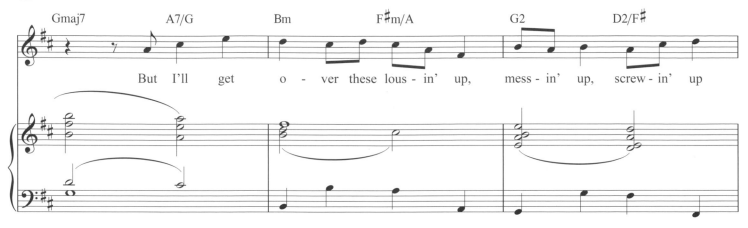

But I'll get o - ver these lous - in' up, mess - in' up, screw - in' up

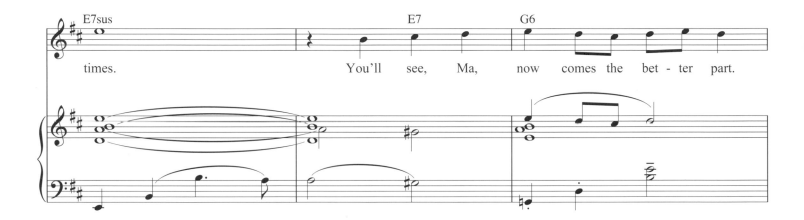

times. You'll see, Ma, now comes the bet - ter part.

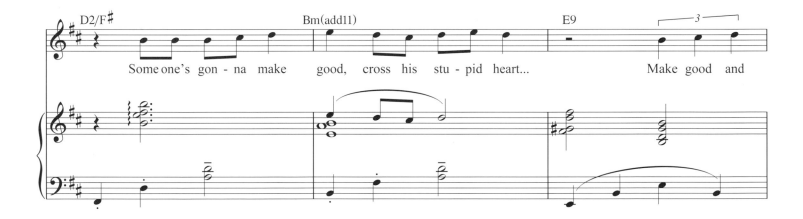

Some one's gon - na make good, cross his stu - pid heart... Make good and

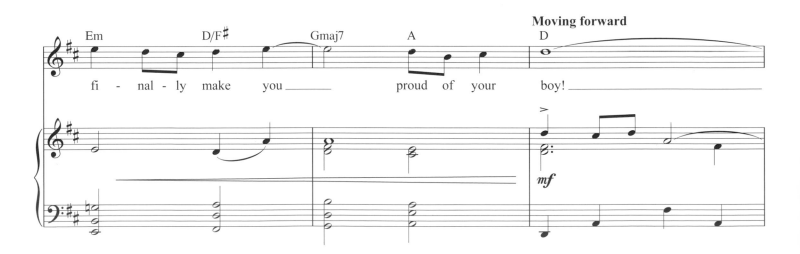

fi - nal - ly make you _____ proud of your boy! _____

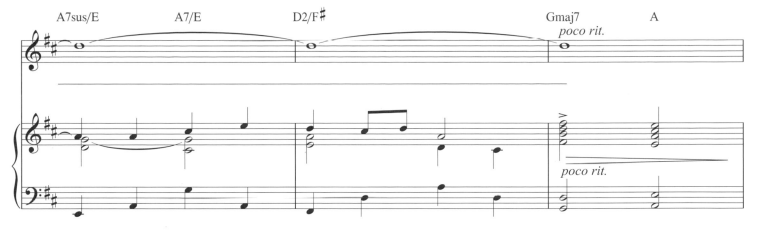

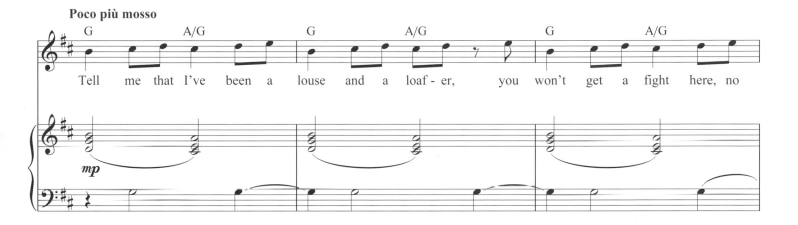

Poco più mosso

Tell me that I've been a louse and a loaf-er, you won't get a fight here, no

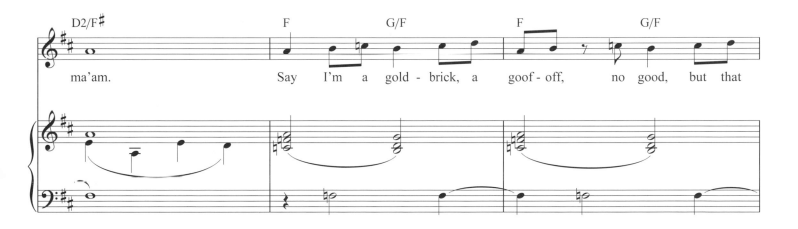

ma'am. Say I'm a gold-brick, a goof-off, no good, but that

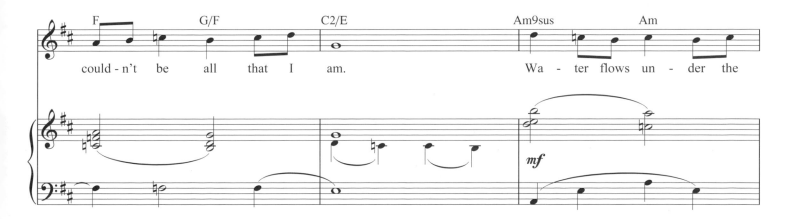

could-n't be all that I am. Wa-ter flows un-der the

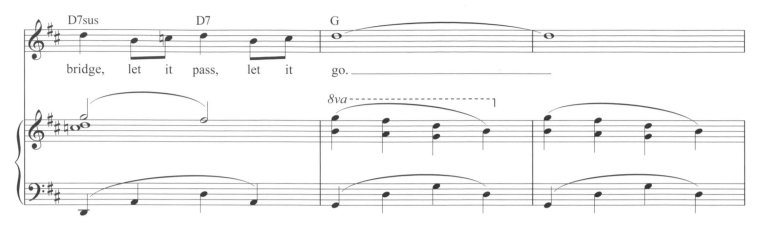

bridge, let it pass, let it go. _____

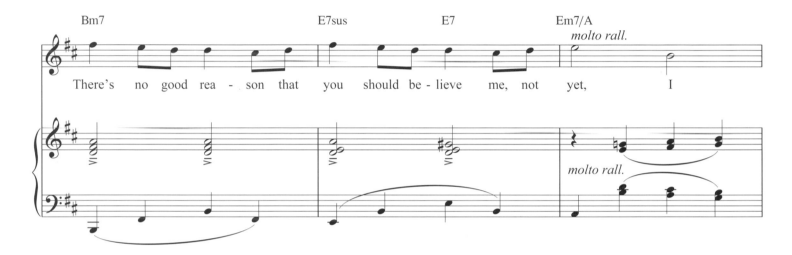

There's no good rea - son that you should be - lieve me, not yet, I

know, but... Some - day and soon, I'll make you

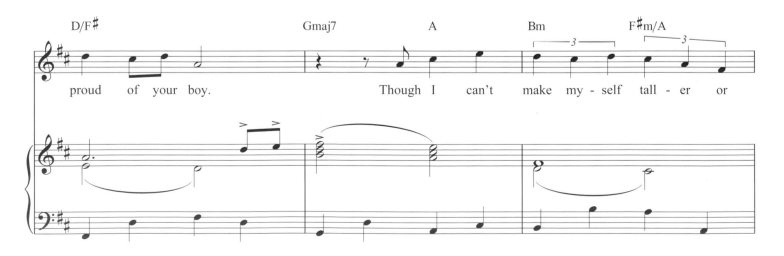

proud of your boy. Though I can't make my - self tall - er or

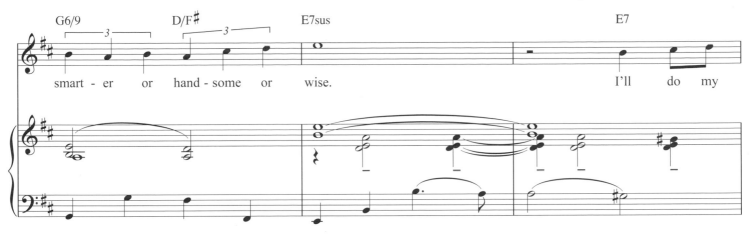

smart-er or hand-some or wise.
I'll do my

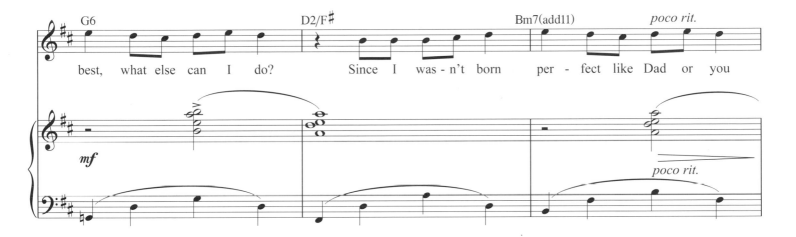

best, what else can I do? Since I was-n't born per-fect like Dad or you

Freely

Mom, I will try to, try hard to make you proud of your

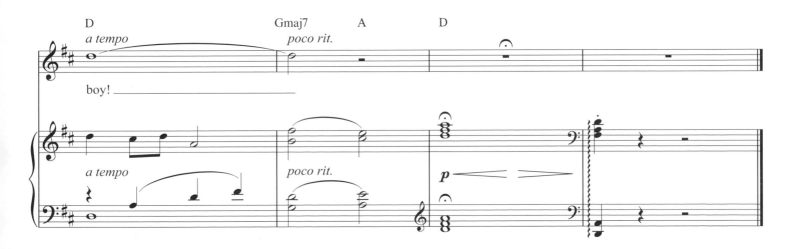

boy! _____

EVERMORE
from *Beauty and the Beast*

Music by Alan Menken
Lyrics by Tim Rice

Moderately slow, with freedom

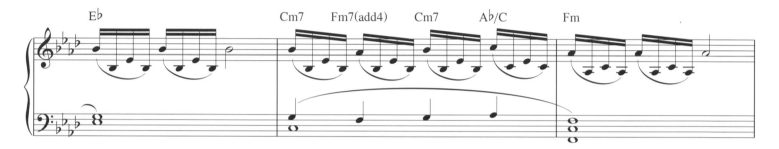

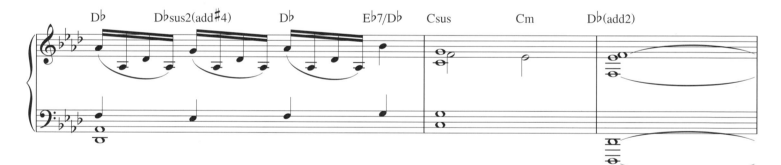

Sturdy Ballad ♩ = 99

BEAST:

I was the one_ who had it all;___

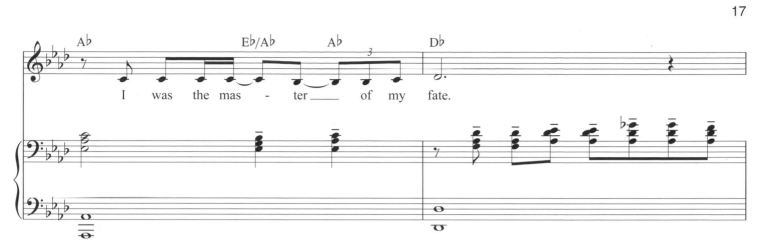

I was the mas - ter ___ of my fate.

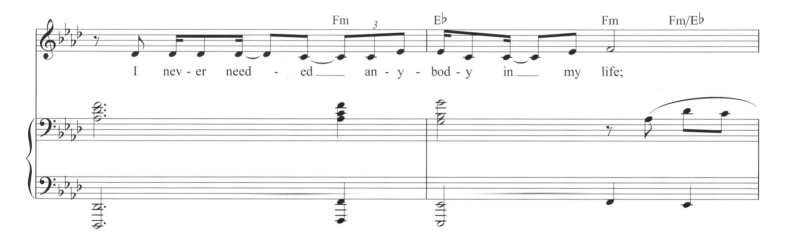

I nev - er need - ed ___ an - y - bod - y in ___ my life;

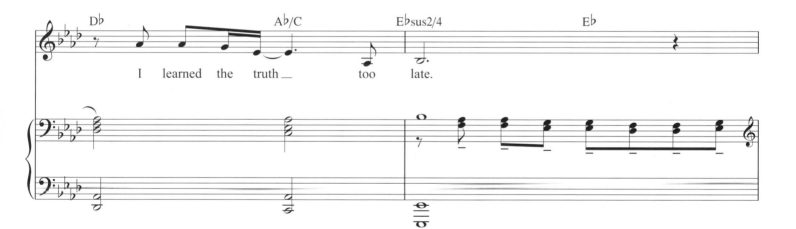

I learned the truth ___ too late.

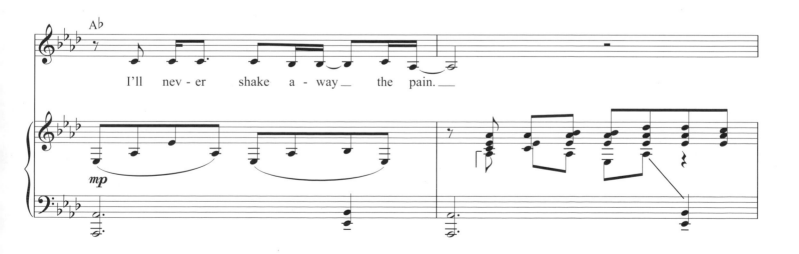

I'll nev - er shake a - way ___ the pain. ___

I close my eyes, _ but _ she's still there.

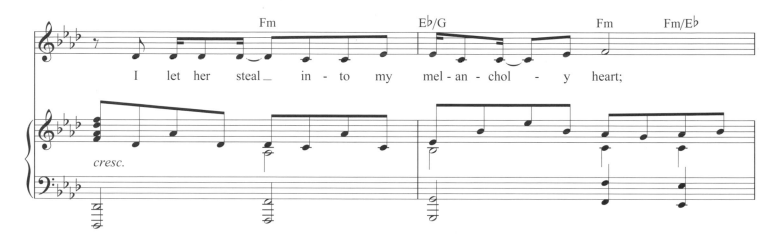

I let her steal _ in - to my mel - an - chol - y heart;

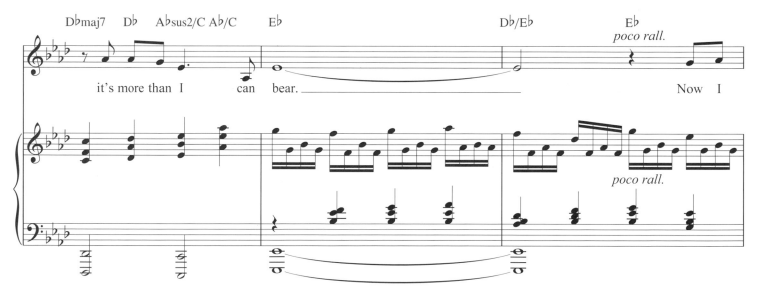

it's more than I can bear. _____ Now I

Poco più mosso ♩ = 104

know she'll nev - er leave me, e - ven as she runs a -

way. She will still tor-ment me, calm me, hurt me, move

me, come what may.

A little faster

Wast-ing in my lone-ly

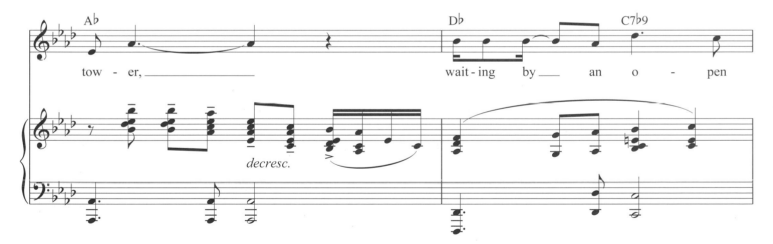

tow-er,   wait-ing by an o-pen

decresc.

A little slower

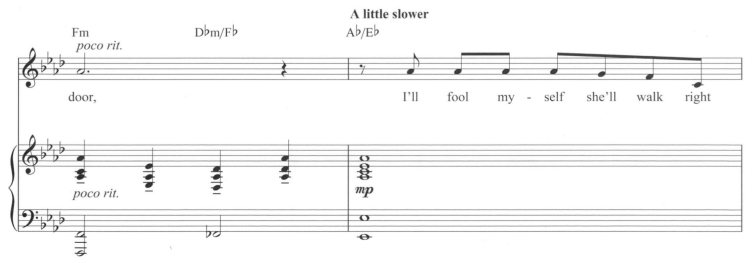

door,   I'll fool my-self she'll walk right

poco rit.

poco rit.

mp

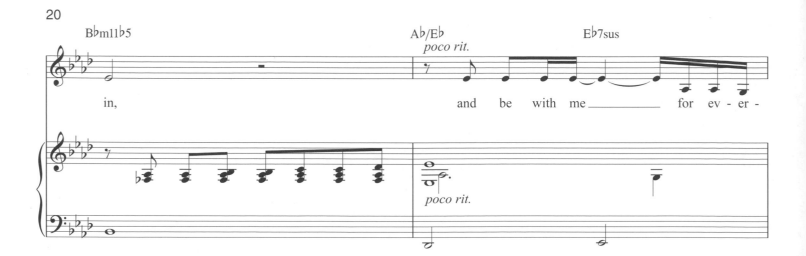

in,   and be with me _____ for ev - er -

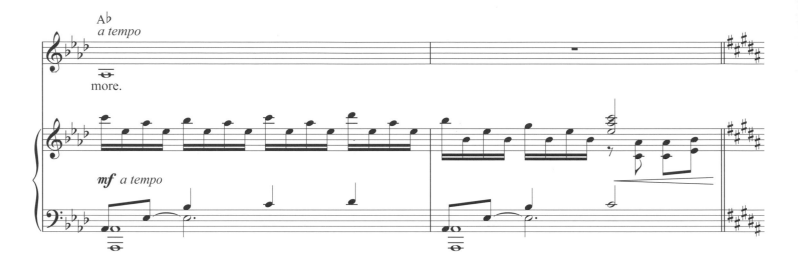

more.

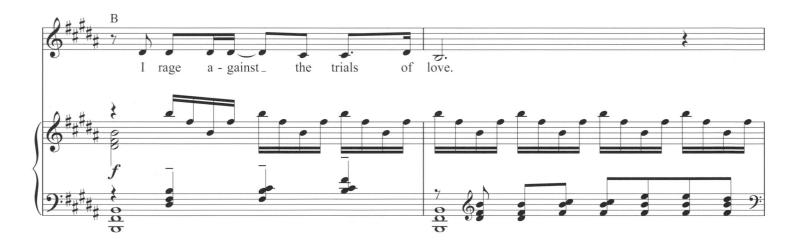

I rage a - gainst _ the trials of love.

I curse the fad - ing ____ of the light.

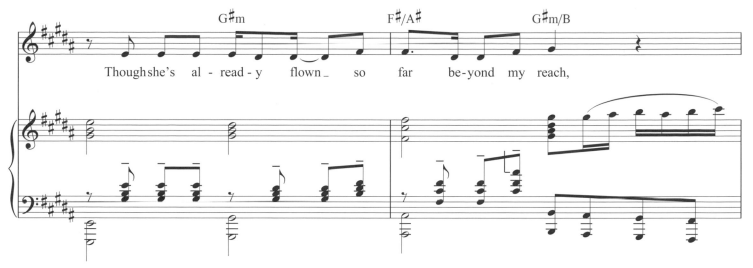

Though she's al-read-y flown so far be-yond my reach,

she's nev-er out of sight.

Now I know she'll nev-er leave me, e-ven

as she fades from view. She will still in-spire me,

be a part _ of ev-'ry-thing _ I do.

Wast-ing in my lone - ly tow-er,   wait-ing by an o - pen

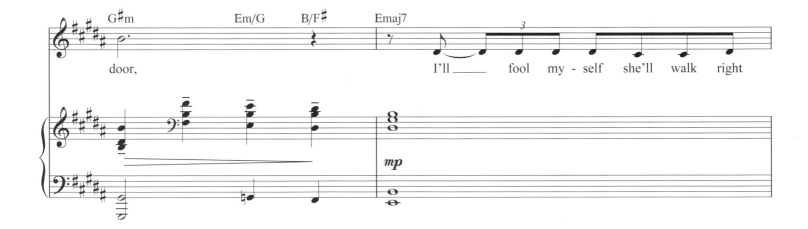

door,   I'll ___ fool my-self she'll walk right

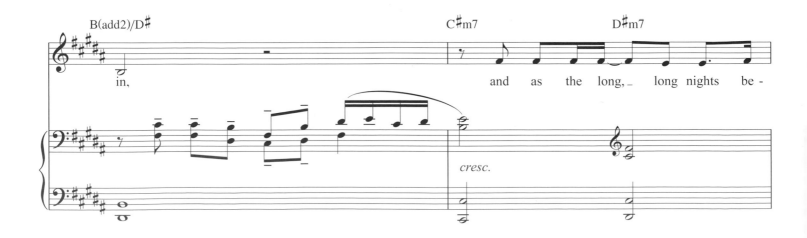

in,   and as the long, _ long nights be-

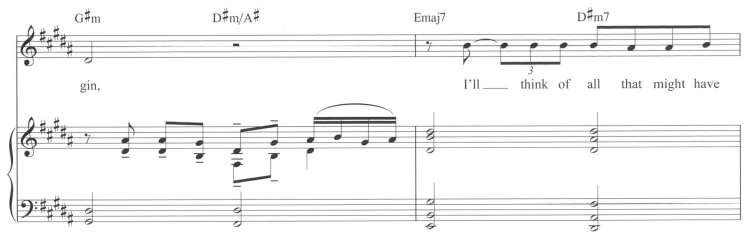

gin,

I'll___ think of all that might have

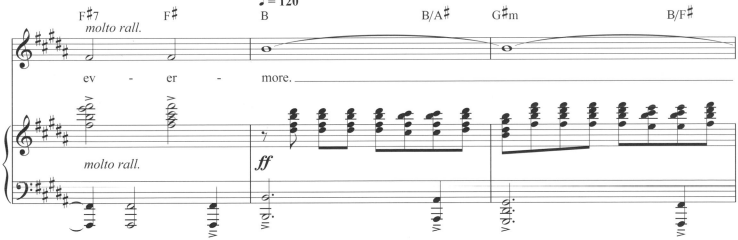

been,

wait - ing here

for

ev - er - more.___

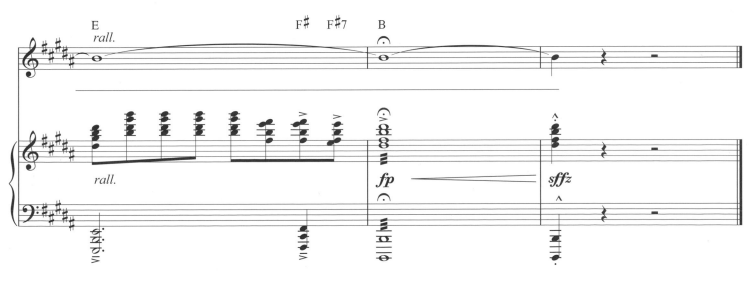

PROUD CORAZÓN

from *Coco*

Music by Germaine Franco
Lyrics by Adrian Molina

Moderately

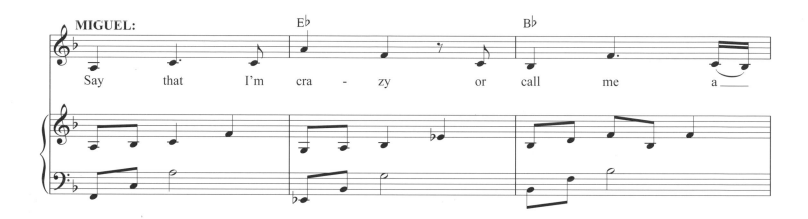

MIGUEL:

Say that I'm cra - zy or call me a _____

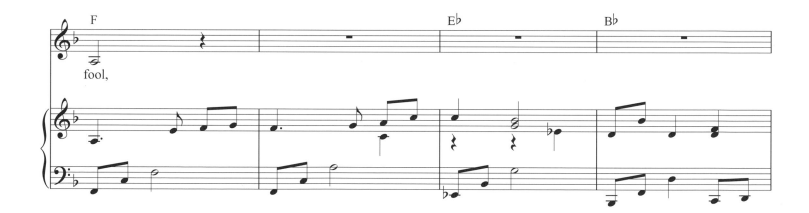

fool,

but last night it seemed _____ that I

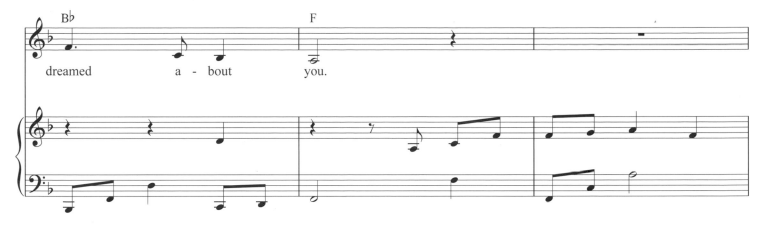

dreamed a - bout you.

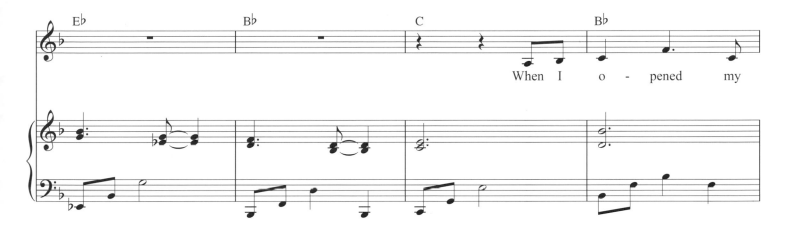

When I o - pened my

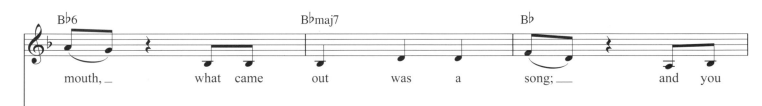

mouth, __ what came out was a song; __ and you

knew ev - 'ry word, __ and we all sang __ a -

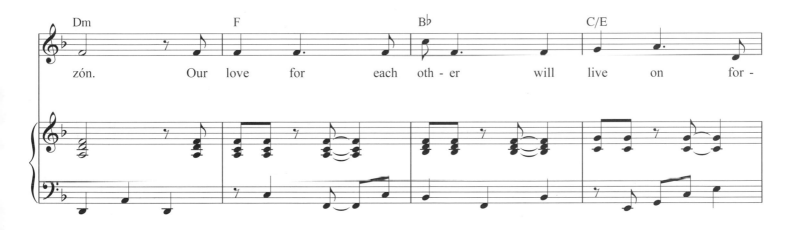

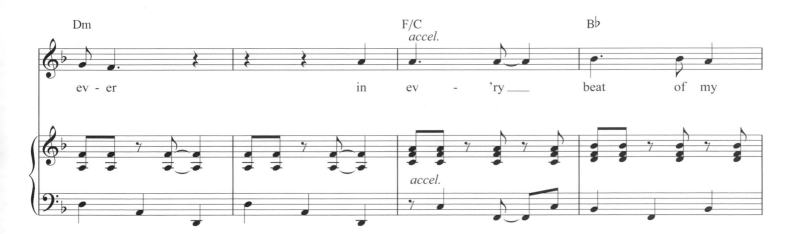

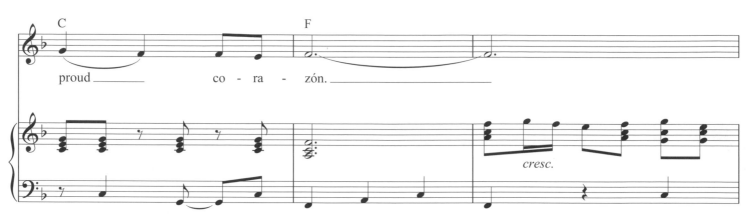

Moderately, in 1

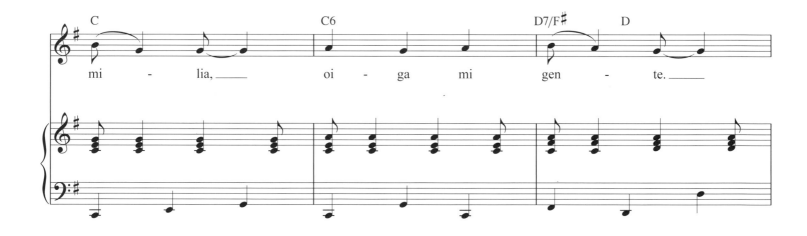

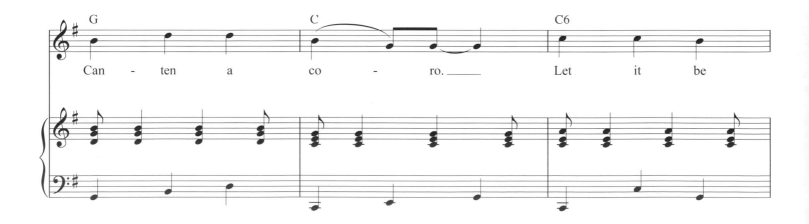

known: _ Our love for each oth-er will

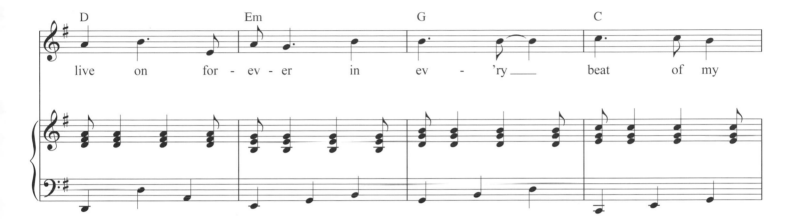

live on for-ev-er in ev-'ry ___ beat of my

proud ___ co-ra-zón.   proud ___ co-ra-

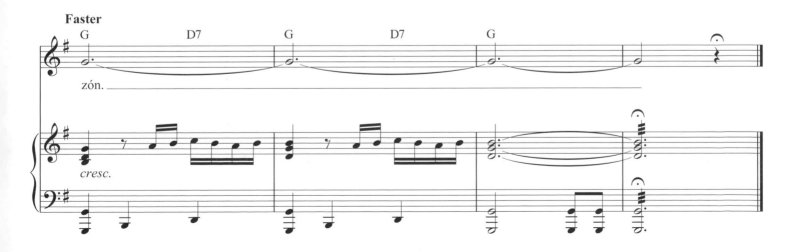

zón. ___

REMEMBER ME
(Ernesto de la Cruz)
from *Coco*

Music and Lyrics by Kristen Anderson-Lopez
and Robert Lopez

even if I'm far a-way,_ I hold you in my heart. I sing a se-cret song to you each

night we are a-part. Re-mem - ber me, though I have to trav-el far._ Re-mem - ber

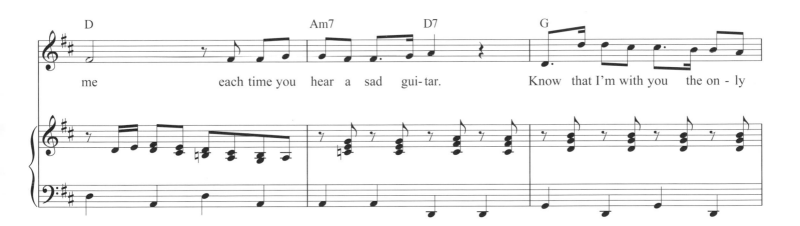

me each time you hear a sad gui-tar. Know that I'm with you the on - ly

way that I can be. Un - til you're in my arms a - gain, re-mem - ber

* An interlude has been cut for this edition.

night we are a-part. Re-mem - ber me, though I have to trav-el far._ Re-mem - ber

me each time you hear a sad gui-tar. Know that I'm with you the on - ly

Slowly, deliberately

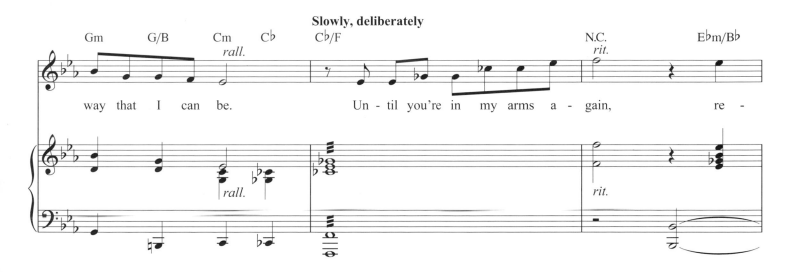

way that I can be. Un - til you're in my arms a - gain, re -

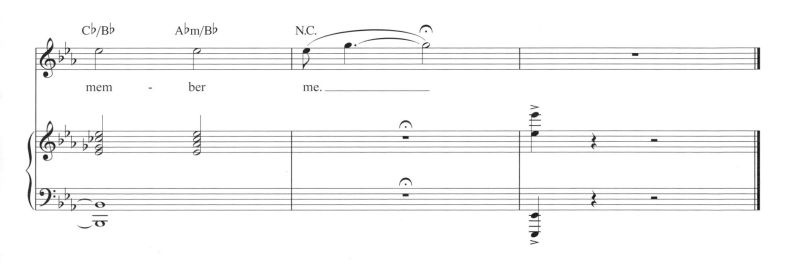

mem - ber me._

IN SUMMER
from The Broadway Musical *Frozen*

Music and Lyrics by Kristen Anderson-Lopez
and Robert Lopez

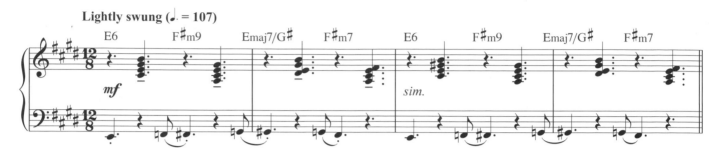

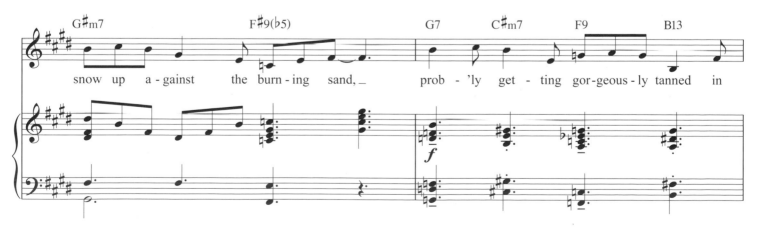

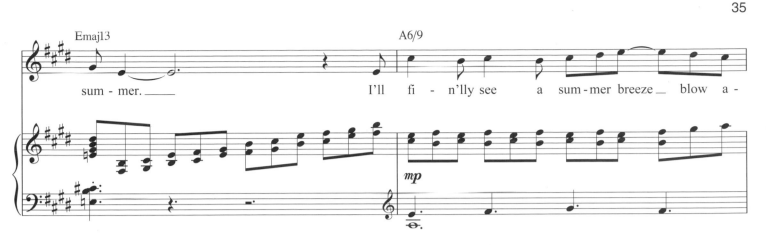

sum - mer. _____ I'll fi - n'lly see a sum - mer breeze blow a-

way a win - ter storm _ and find out what hap-pens to sol - id wa-ter when it gets warm. _

And I can't wait to see what my bud-dies all think of me. Just i-

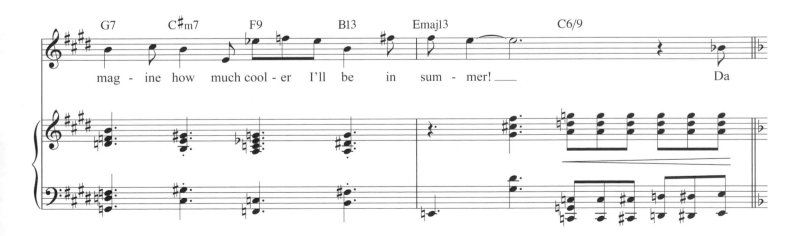

mag - ine how much cool - er I'll be in sum - mer! _____ Da

da   da doo   ba ba ba ba ba - ba boo. __   The hot and the cold are both so in-tense.

Put 'em to-geth er, it just makes sense!   Rat da dat da da da da da da da doo. __

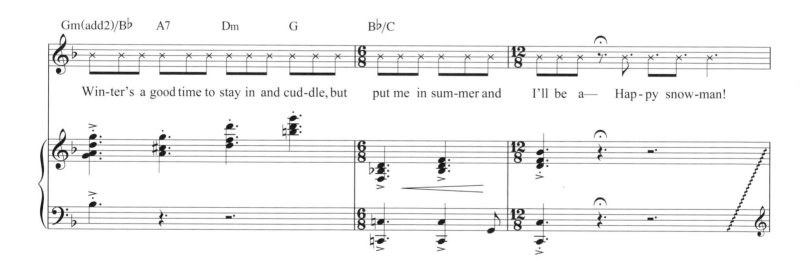

Win-ter's a good time to stay in and cud-dle, but   put me in sum-mer and   I'll be a— Hap - py snow-man!

When life gets rough   I like to hold on __ to my dream   of re -

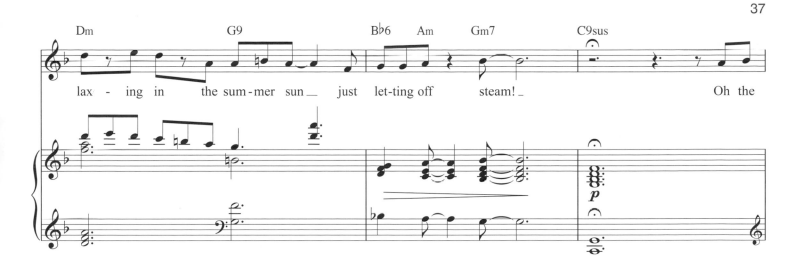

lax - ing in the sum-mer sun __ just let-ting off steam! __ Oh the

Slower

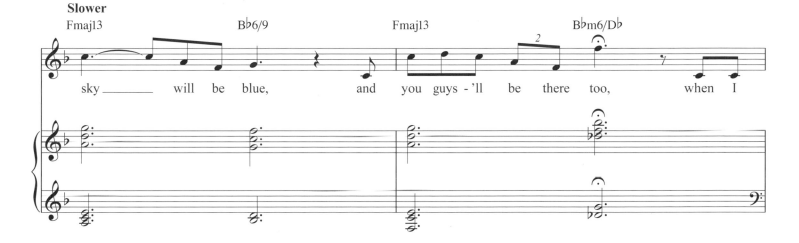

sky _____ will be blue, and you guys - 'll be there too, when I

fi - nal - ly do what fro-zen things do in sum-mer!

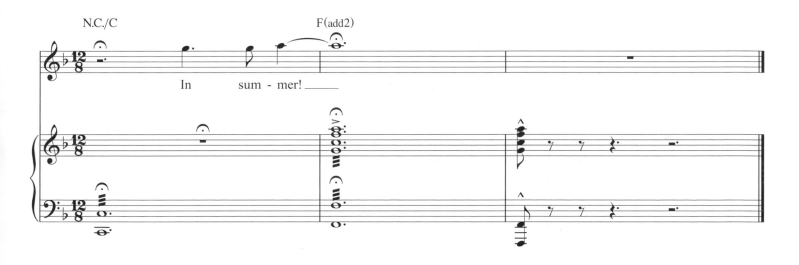

In sum - mer! _____

WHEN I AM OLDER

from *Frozen 2*

Music and Lyrics by Kristen Anderson-Lopez
and Robert Lopez

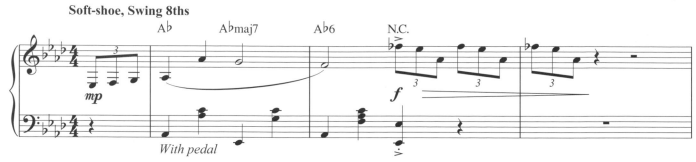

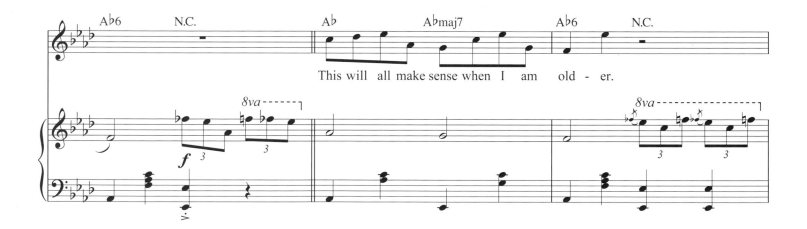

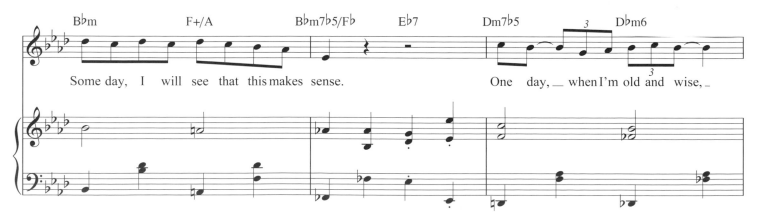

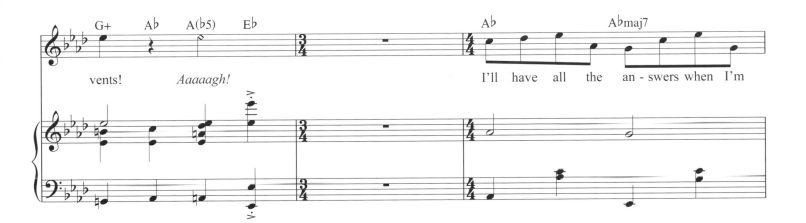

I'll think back and re-al-ize___ that these were all com-plete-ly nor-mal e-

vents! *Aaaaagh!* I'll have all the an-swers when I'm

old-er! Like, why we're in this dark, en-chant-ed wood.

I know___ in a cou-ple years,___ these will seem like child-ish fears,___ and

so I know, this is-n't bad, it's good! *Excuse me.*

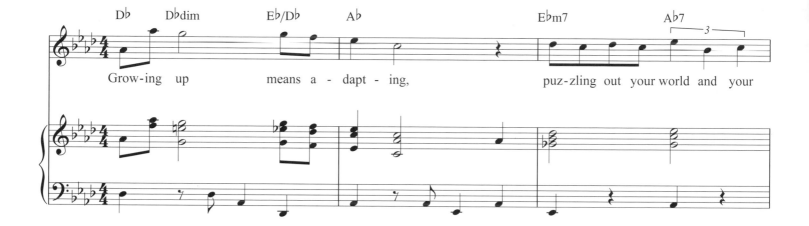

Grow-ing up means a - dapt - ing, puz-zling out your world and your

place! When I'm more ma-ture, I'll feel to - tal - ly se - cure be-ing

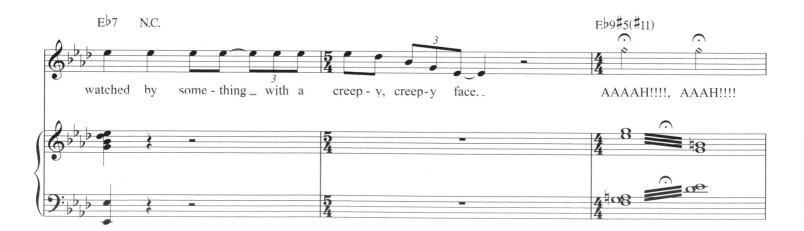

watched by some-thing __ with a creep-y, creep-y face. __ AAAAH!!!!, AAAH!!!!

LOST IN THE WOODS
from *Frozen 2*

Music and Lyrics by Kristen Anderson-Lopez
and Robert Lopez

Moderately, in 2

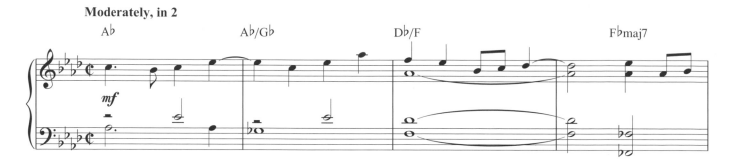

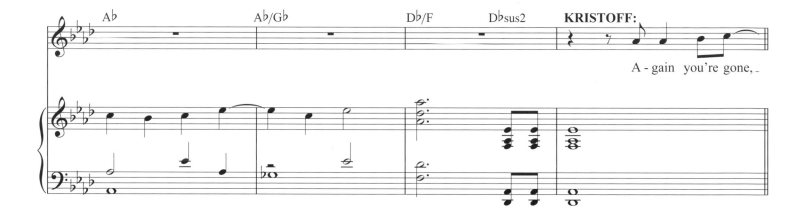

A - gain you're gone, ___

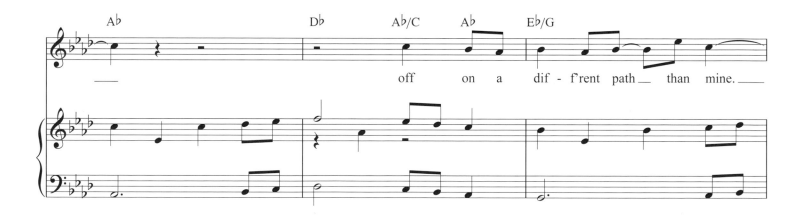

___ off on a dif - f'rent path __ than mine. ___

___ I'm left be - hind, ___ won - der - ing if I should fol -

low. You had to go, and of

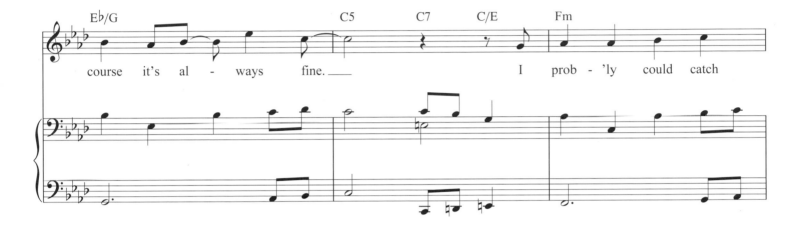

course it's al - ways fine. I prob - 'ly could catch

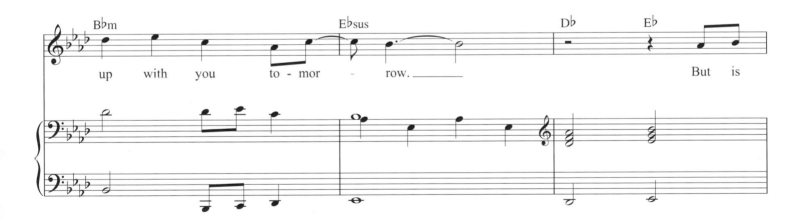

up with you to - mor - row. But is

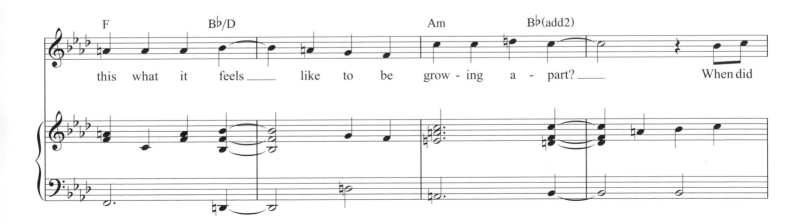

this what it feels like to be grow - ing a - part? When did

I be-come the one___ who's al-ways chas-ing your heart?___ Now I

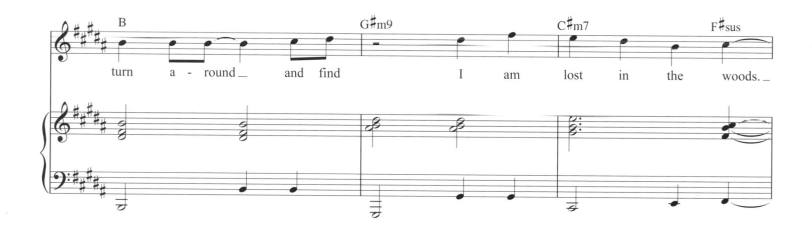

turn a-round___ and find I am lost in the woods.___

North is south, right is left when you're___ gone.___

I'm the one___ who sees you home, but now I'm lost in the woods, ___

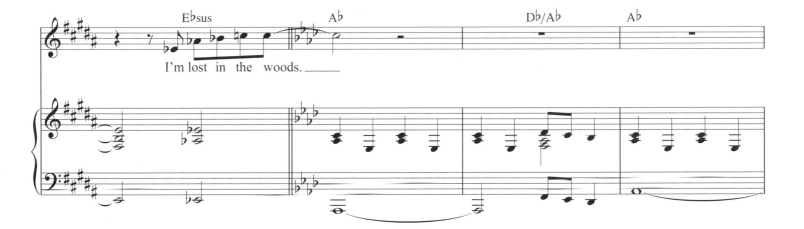

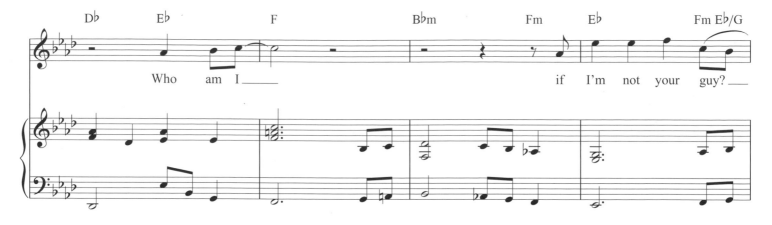

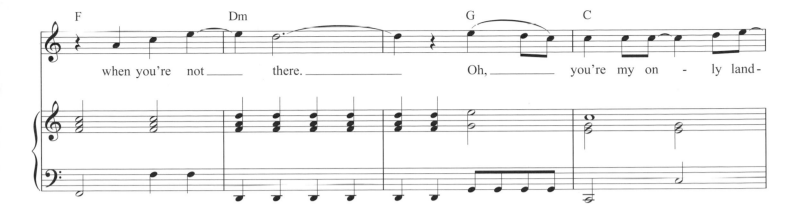

when you're not ____ there. ____ Oh, ____ you're my on - ly land-

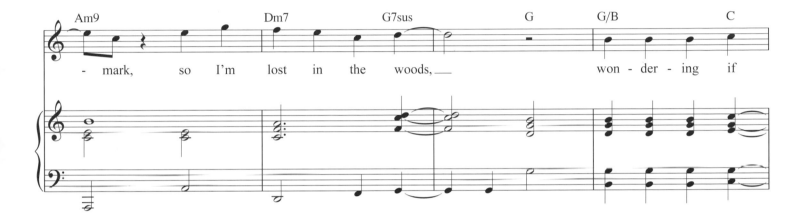

- mark, so I'm lost in the woods, ____ won - der - ing if

you still care. But I'll wait ____

for a sign ____ that I'm ____ your ____ path,

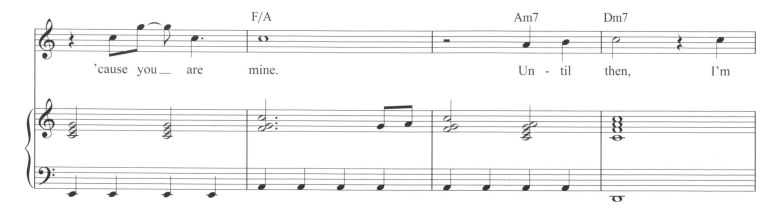

'cause you __ are mine. Un - til then, I'm

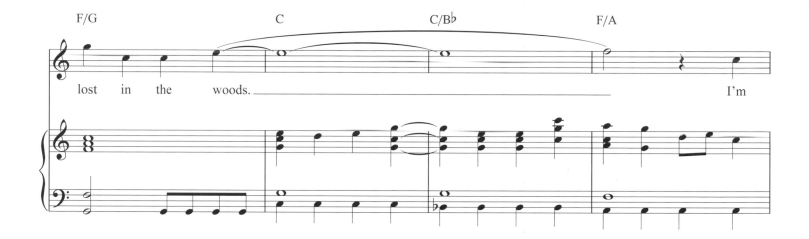

lost in the woods. _____ I'm

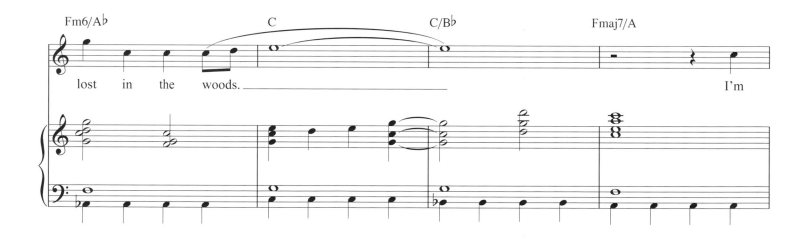

lost in the woods. _____ I'm

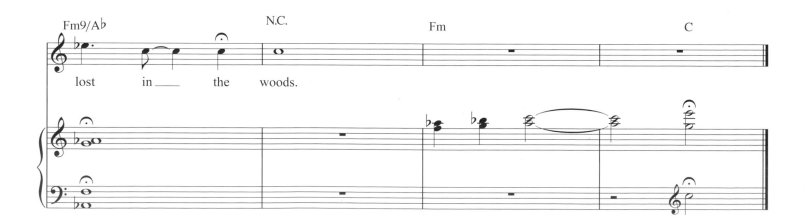

lost in __ the woods.

A CONVERSATION
from *Mary Poppins Returns*

Music by Marc Shaiman
Lyrics by Scott Wittman and Marc Shaiman

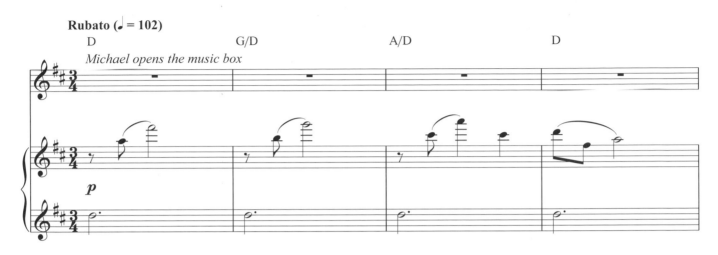

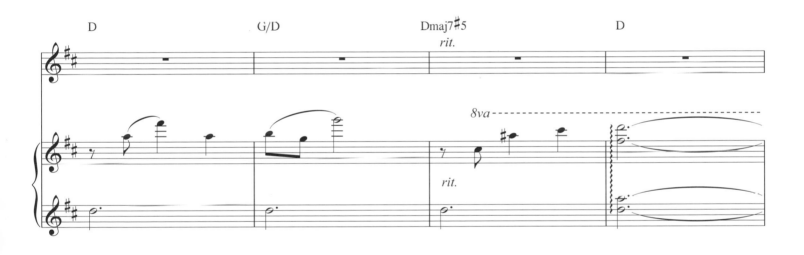

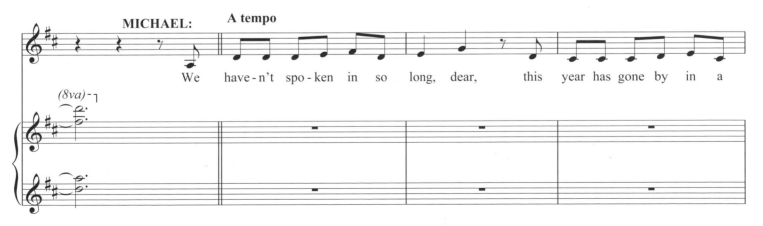

MICHAEL: We haven't spo-ken in so long, dear, this year has gone by in a

blur. To - day seems ev - 'ry-thing's gone wrong here, I'm look - ing for the way things

were. I know you'd laugh and call me trag - ic _____ for

ev - 'ry-thing's in dis - ar - ray. These rooms were al - ways full of mag - ic that's

van-ished since you went a - way. _____

In time, slightly faster (♩ = c. 105)

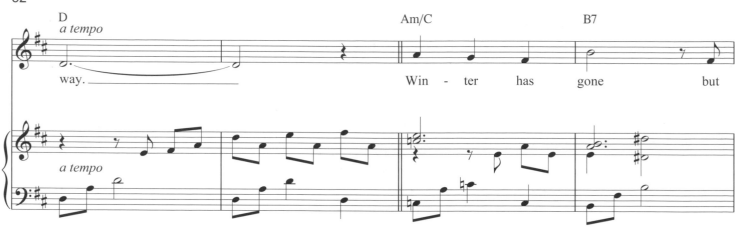

way. _____ Winter has gone but

not from this room, snow's left the lane but the

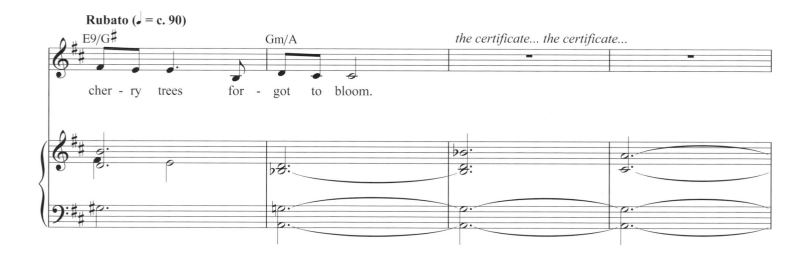

cher - ry trees for - got to bloom. *the certificate... the certificate...*

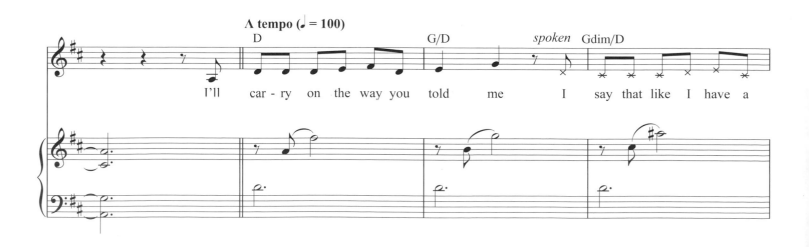

I'll car - ry on the way you told me I say that like I have a

choice. And though you are not here to hold me, in the ech-oes I can hear your

voice. But still one ques-tion fills my day, dear, _ the an-swer I've most longed to

know. Each mo-ment since you went a-way, dear, the ques-tion, Kate, is

where'd you go?

(Underneath the)
LOVELY LONDON SKY
from *Mary Poppins Returns*

Music by Marc Shaiman
Lyrics by Scott Wittman and Marc Shaiman

When the ear-ly morn-ing hours have come and gone

with the mist-y morn-ing showers I greet the dawn, _____ for

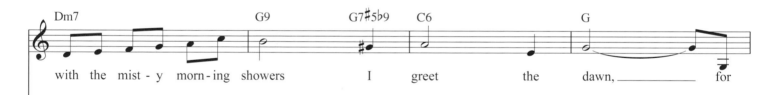

when the sun has hit the ground_____ there's lots of trea-sures to be found

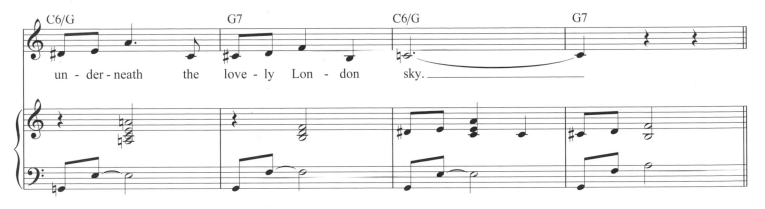

un - der - neath the love - ly Lon - don sky.

Though the lamps I'm turn - ing down, please don't feel

blue, _____ for in this part of Lon - don town the light shines

through. Don't be - lieve the things you've read, _____ you

never know what's up a-head — under-neath the

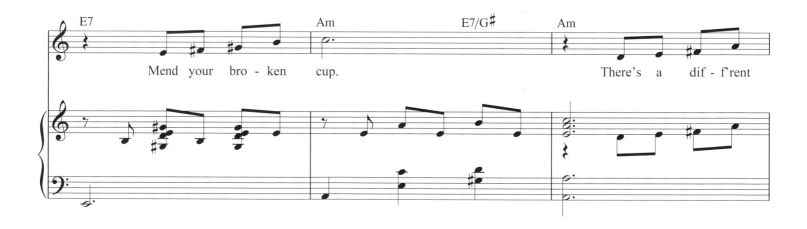

love-ly Lon-don sky. Have a pot of tea.

Mend your bro-ken cup. There's a dif-f'rent

point of view a-wait-ing you if you would just look up! I know

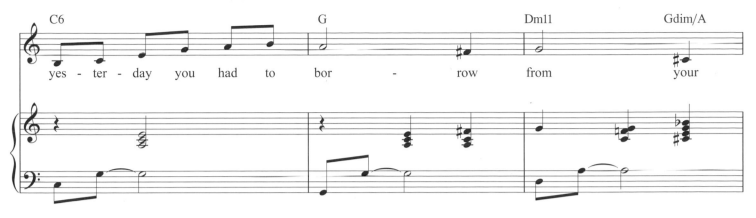

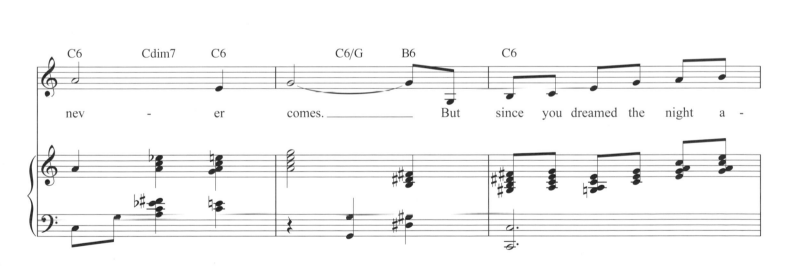

count your bless - ings, you're a luck - y guy

for you're un - der -neath the love - ly Lon - don sky.

(whistle) -

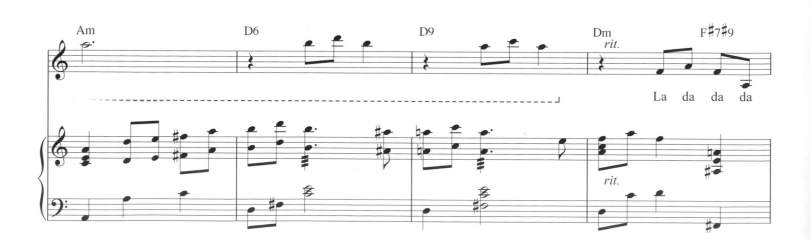

La da da da

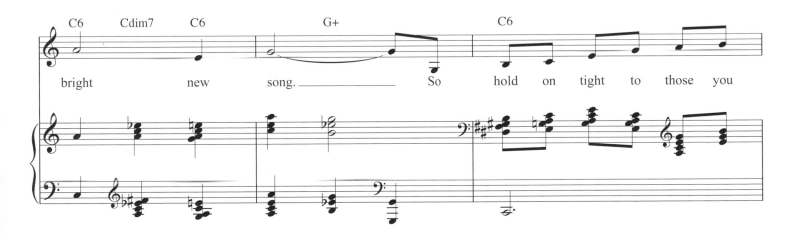

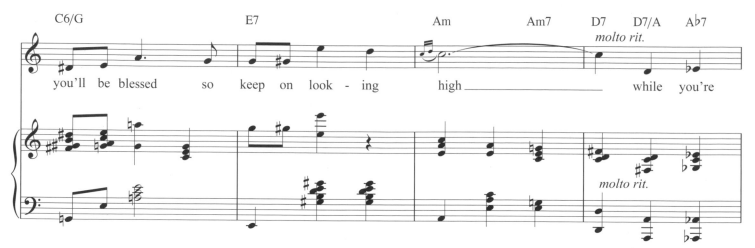

you'll be blessed so keep on look - ing high _____ while you're

un - der - neath the love - ly Lon - don sky. _____

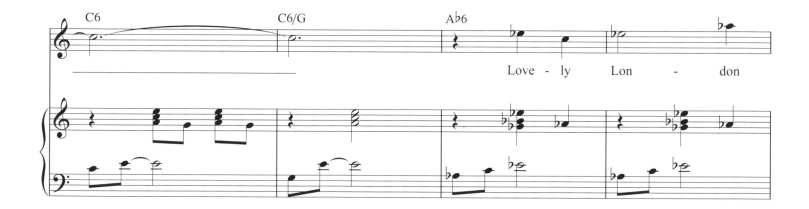

Love - ly Lon - don

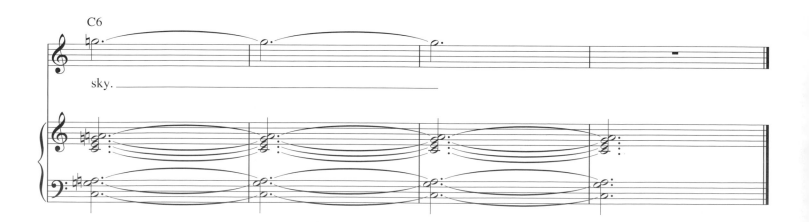

sky. _____

YOU'RE WELCOME
from *Moana*

Music and Lyrics by
Lin-Manuel Miranda

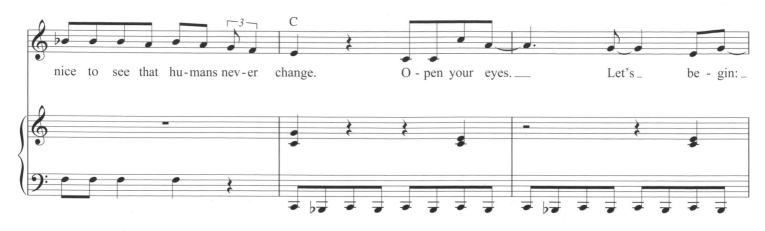

nice to see that hu-mans nev-er change. O - pen your eyes. ___ Let's _ be - gin: _

___ Yes, it's real - ly me, it's Mau - i. Breathe it in,

I know it's a lot: ___ the hair, _ the bod, ___ when you're

star - ing at a dem - i - god. ___ What can I say ___

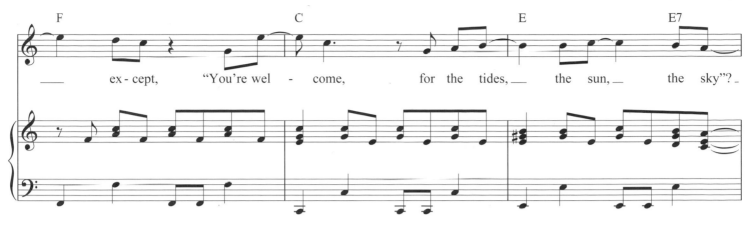

ex - cept, "You're wel - come, for the tides, ___ the sun, ___ the sky"? ___

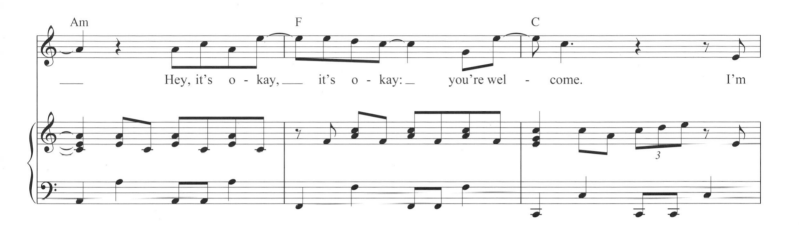

___ Hey, it's o - kay, ___ it's o - kay: ___ you're wel - come. I'm

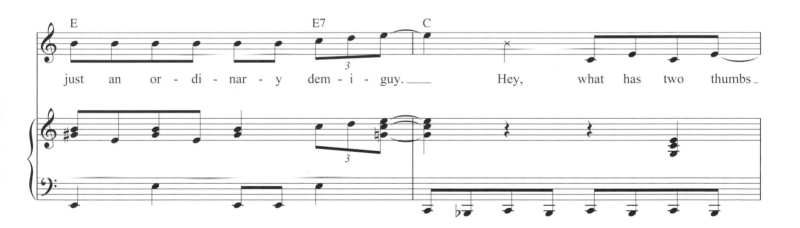

just an or - di - nar - y dem - i - guy. ___ Hey, what has two thumbs ___

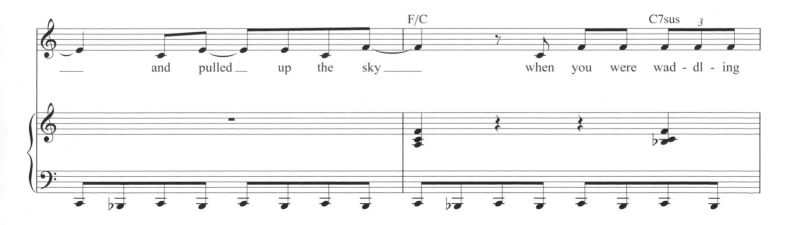

___ and pulled ___ up the sky ___ when you were wad - dl - ing

yea high? This guy! When the nights got cold, ___ who stole ___ you fire ___

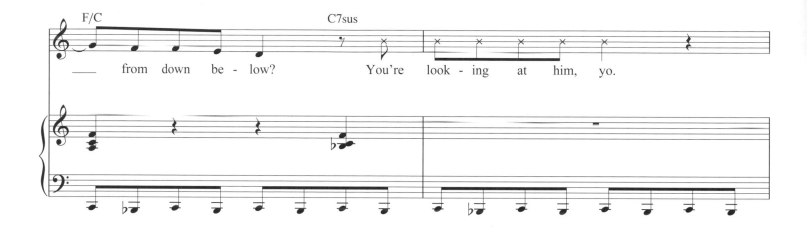

___ from down be - low? You're look - ing at him, yo.

Oh, al - so, I las - soed ___ the sun. ___ You're wel-come. ...To

stretch your days and bring you fun. ___ Al - so, I har -

-nessed _ the breeze. You're wel-come. ...To fill your sails and shake your trees. _

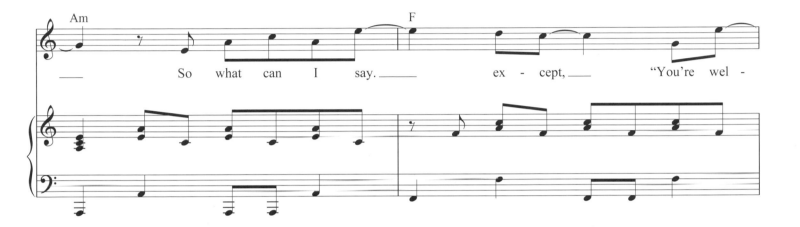

_ So what can I say. _ ex - cept, _ "You're wel -

- come, for the is - lands I pulled _ from the sea?" _

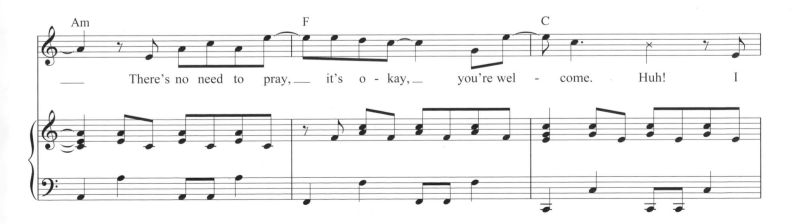

_ There's no need to pray, _ it's o - kay, _ you're wel - come. Huh! I

guess it's just my way of be-ing me! ___ You're wel - come! You're wel -

- come! Well, come to think of it:

Kid, hon-est-ly, I could go on and on. I could ex-plain ev-'ry nat-'ral phe-nom-e-non.

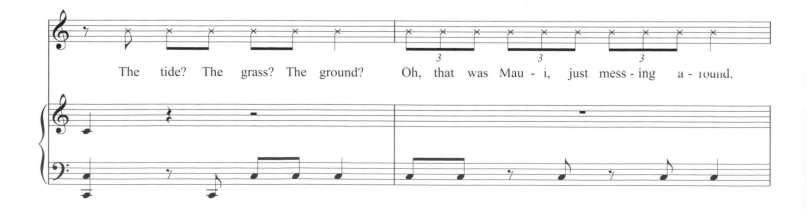

The tide? The grass? The ground? Oh, that was Mau - i, just mess-ing a - round.

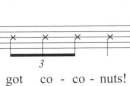

I killed an eel, I bur - ied its guts, sprout - ed a tree: now you got co - co - nuts!

What's the les - son? What is the take - a - way? Don't mess with Mau - i when he's on a break - a - way.

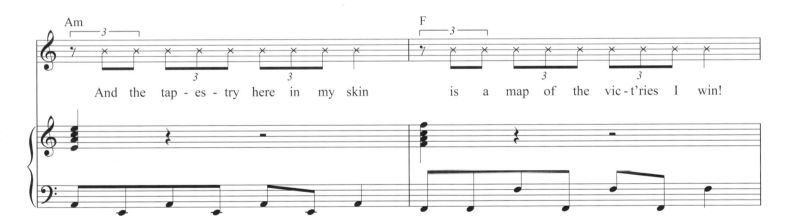

And the tap - es - try here in my skin is a map of the vic - t'ries I win!

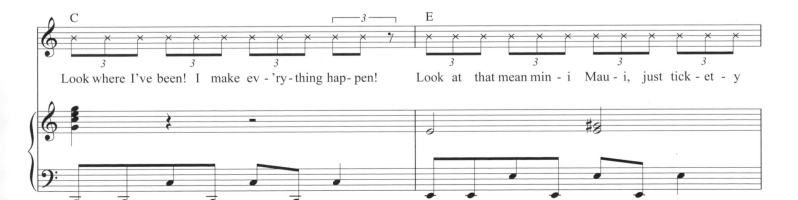

Look where I've been! I make ev - 'ry - thing hap - pen! Look at that mean min - i Mau - i, just tick - et - y

tapp - in'! Heh, heh, heh, heh, heh, heh, hey!

Well, an - y - way, ___ let me say, ___ "You're wel - come, for the won -
(You're wel - come.)

- der - ful world you know." ___ Hey, it's o - kay, ___ it's o - kay: ___ you're wel -
(Ha, ha, ha.)

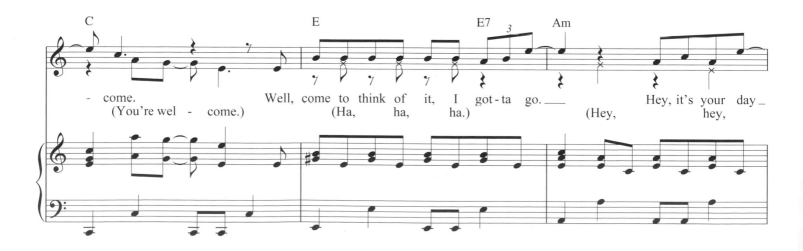

- come. Well, come to think of it, I got - ta go. ___ Hey, it's your day ___
(You're wel - come.) (Ha, ha, ha.) (Hey, hey,

to say, __ "You're wel - come," 'cause I'm gon-na need__ that boat.__
hey, hey!) (You're wel - come.) (Ha, ha, ha, ha.)

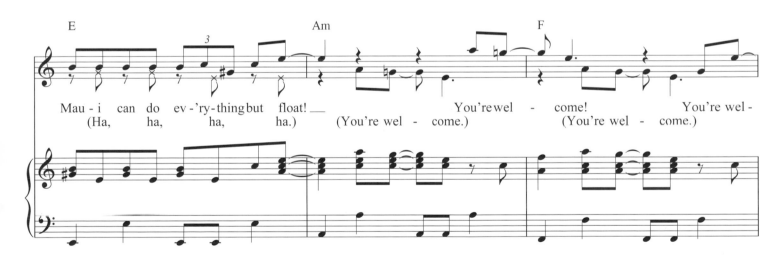

__ I'm sail-ing a - way, __ a - way.__ You're wel - come, 'cause
(Hey, hey, hey, hey.) (You're wel - come.)

Mau - i can do ev - 'ry-thing but float! __ You're wel - come! You're wel -
(Ha, ha, ha, ha.) (You're wel - come.) (You're wel - come.)

- come! __ And thank you.

NEVER TOO LATE

from *The Lion King 2019*

Music by Elton John
Lyrics by Tim Rice

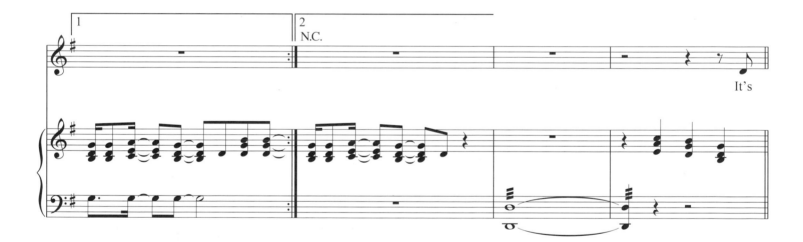

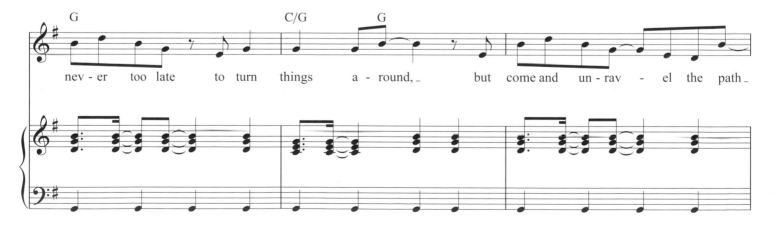

nev-er too late to turn things a-round,_ but come and un-rav-el the path_

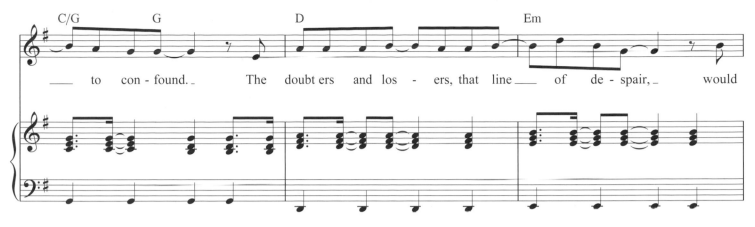

to con-found. The doubt-ers and los-ers, that line of de-spair, would

tell you it's o-ver, you're go-ing no-where. It's nev-er too late, I hope,

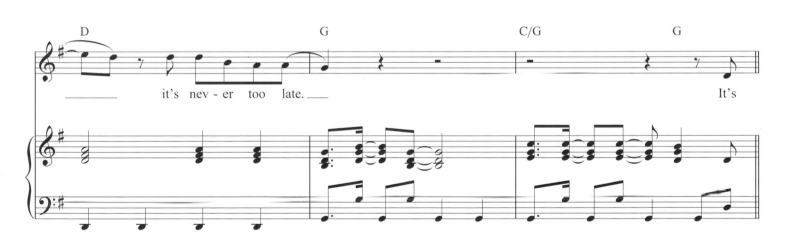

it's nev-er too late. It's

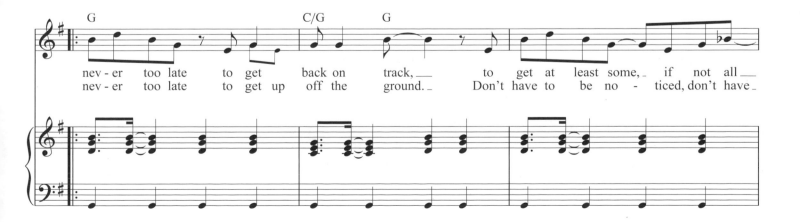

nev-er too late to get back on track, to get at least some, if not all
nev-er too late to get up off the ground. Don't have to be no-ticed, don't have

of it back. I thought I was hap - py, and some-times I was, but
to be crowned. I did what I've done, and I don't try to hide. I

sad-ness is just as im-por - tant be-cause, got to car - ry the weight and hope
lost man - y things, but nev - er my pride. It's nev - er too late, I know,

it's nev - er too late.
it's nev - er too late.

Nev-er too late to fight the fight. Nev-er too late to cheat the night. Nev-er too late to win the day.

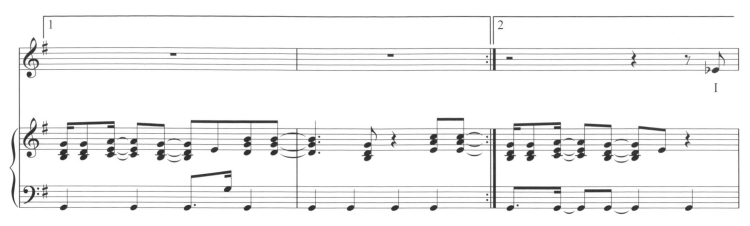

used to say, "I don't have time, I'm sleep-ing to - night." _ A day do - in' noth - in' is

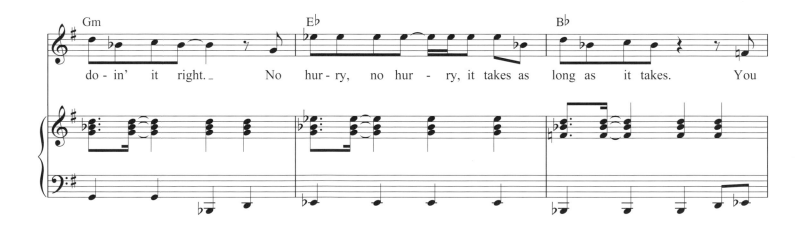

do - in' it right. _ No hur - ry, no hur - ry, it takes as long as it takes. You

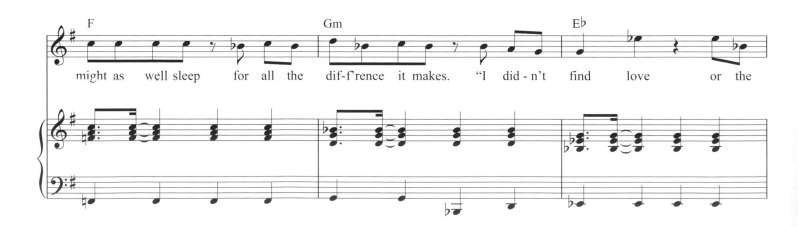

might as well sleep for all the dif-f'rence it makes. "I did - n't find love or the

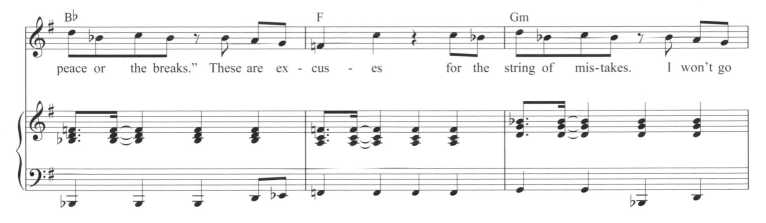

peace or the breaks." These are ex - cus - es for the string of mis-takes. I won't go

back there. Not go-ing back there.

Nev-er too late to fight the fight. Nev-er too late to cheat the night.

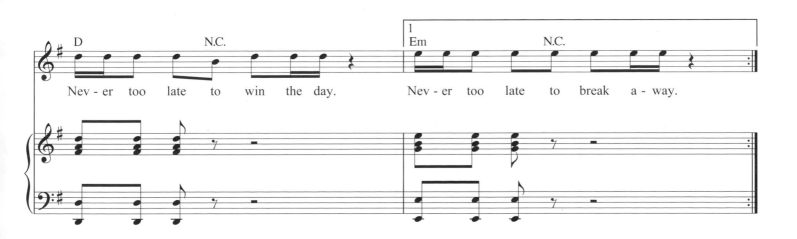

Nev - er too late to win the day. Nev - er too late to break a - way.

Nev-er too late to break a-way. Time is not to move too fast, but time is not my friend. I'm a

long way from the start, but fur-ther from the end. ___ Oh, ___

it's nev-er too late. ___ It's nev-er too late. _

___ Oh! It's nev-er too late. ___

It's nev - er too late. ___

It's nev - er too late. ___

G   C/G   G

___ *(Vocal ad lib.)*

(2nd time only)

1   2   N.C.